Chicktime

www.chicktime.com

Encouraging women to develop their passions
and use their gifts to make the world a better place for
the next generation!

Lori Rhodes

THIRD EDITION

Safari Multimedia, LLC

Lori Rhodes is the founder of Chicktime, Inc. and the Chicktime Canyon Lake chapter. To contact Lori email her at info@chicktime.com

Chicktime, Inc. is a 501(c)(3) Public Charity.

TO JOIN A CHAPTER:
We make it easy, all women are welcome. Visit www.chicktime.com

TO ATTEND A CHICKTIME EVENT:
Online calendar and registration at chicktime.com

TO START A NEW CHAPTER:
After reading this book, contact info@chicktime.com

Visit Chicktime.com to join the Chicktime movement. Impact the next generation and change your life!

Published by Safari Imprint

For information: info@chicktime.com

www.chicktime.com

ISBN: 978-0615727660

Artwork by Carolyn Boden
Book design by Safari Multimedia, LLC.

What is Chicktime?

Chicktime is a movement empowering women to stop the cycle of child abuse by going into children's homes/shelters and loving on the kids. We believe that if a child is convinced they are loved their wounds will heal, and they won't lash out when they are adults and repeat the cycle of abuse with their own children. We do this by setting up monthly activities with children living in children's homes and encouraging women in the local community to come in and teach classes based on their passions.

We invite volunteers to come in and play along with the kids during the activities acting as the fun aunt or big sister… just a way of bonding with them and showing them love through time and attention. The hope is that the volunteers will connect with the kids and find ways to come back and help out more with needs the children's homes have. Chicktime is a gateway to start up the relationships.

To my family.
Without your love, support and encouragement
Chicktime would not exist.

Contents

Forward

Chicktime is a grass-roots movement meant to support and encourage women pursuing their passions with gusto. It is our belief that if each woman on the planet right now takes her place we can together accomplish the phenomenal.

We help passionate women set up Chicktime groups in their communities with the hope of having a network of chapters across America. Chicktime groups accomplish many things, here are a few: Connect women to creative and fun opportunities to pursue their passions while serving others, provide a place for women to serve and play together, and raise awareness for local women and children's charities.

Each Chicktime chapter partners with a local charity. A typical Chicktime chapter consists of three core leaders and 12 monthly workshop/activity leaders. You will need one woman to lead the activity each month, based on the Bunco concept! Most chapters grow to 100+ members!

What do the volunteers do who aren't leading the workshop/activity that month? They show up and play!! Each monthly activity/workshop leader identifies her gift – something she loves to do – and turns it into an activity appropriate for the children (or whatever population) your chapter serves (and the women/volunteers who show up to play).

There is so much passion and joy wrapped up in the activity/workshop that everyone present can't help but wonder, "what is my passion... and how can I use it to bring joy to others?" And remember, if you are not the leader that month, as a volunteer, you just show up to assist the leader and play along with the children (or whatever population) your charity serves – guilt-free serving!

The idea is to expose the next generation to a wide array of gifts and talents so that they can look inside themselves and identify their own.

"Pure and lasting religion in the sight of God our Father means that we must care for orphans and widows in their troubles, and refuse to let the world corrupt us."

– James 1:27

Introduction

It is a mistake to try to look too far ahead.
The chain of destiny can only be grasped one link at a time.
– Winston Churchill

I WILL START WITH THE END. For, you see, it wasn't until Chicktime was well underway that I discovered its true impact, and the reason so many women are drawn to this organization. By end I mean the purpose (not the 'final end'), the reason why Chicktime exists. I didn't discover this 'why' until well into the process. The mission of Chicktime is to encourage women to develop their passions and use their gifts to make the world a better place. The mission is broad and beautiful. It forms the basis of how we do what we do: Stop the cycle of abuse.

From the very beginning, I knew I was supposed to somehow create a network of women across the USA to bring love to victims of abuse. But I had no idea how it was going to happen or the deeper reason I was drawn to the mission. I'm often accused of being impatient. This is true, I am. But I wonder, if I had gathered as much information as I could and mapped out the strategy to fulfill the purpose of the organization, would I still have formed Chicktime? My guess is no.

The monumental weight of the problem of child abuse would have crushed me before I even began. So, I focused instead on establishing and building my local chapter by bringing the love of the local community into one children's center serving little girls recovering from untold abuse. At the same time, I built a website and told everyone who would listen that Chicktime was going national someday. I knew that I would use my love of writing to build a relevant website, and my love for people in making the time to train new leaders. It is honestly a good thing that no one asked me the details of how this would play out, because I had no idea. I just knew that it would, and it has. One chapter at a time!

Before we go any further, I encourage you to think about your personal mission, so you too can find something that aligns with the vision you have for your life. If your passion is to make an impact in the lives of victims of abuse, by all means join your local Chicktime chapter or start one. If it is to save Planet Earth, don't just recycle; get involved with an organization doing something collectively. You may stay with the organization, or most likely, it will help move you to the next thing. I'm writing this book because I see the impact Chicktime has on the thousands of women who volunteer with us. I have limited minutes on Planet Earth. We all do. I want to make sure every minute counts. Sharing what I know about bringing life to the soul seems a waste if I only get to share the knowledge with those I am able to personally touch. I want the whole world to know how wonderful life can be – each and every waking moment – when you choose to walk in your life's purpose.

Before we begin, I need to address an issue that comes up often. Chicktime is not an all-Christian organization. I am unapologetically Christian and often refer to my faith in deep conversation. I would think that a book qualifies as deep, so I would like to share a deeply held belief of mine that's based on writings from the Old Testament. Just about everyone knows the story of Moses and the parting of the Red Sea. Some even understand Moses entered the Red Sea fully believing that God would do something on his behalf, so that Moses could fulfill the mission God had given him. His feet got wet before the sea parted. There is also another reference to this kind of faith a few chapters later. Joshua, Moses' successor, inherited the same people Moses led. An enemy army was chasing them when Joshua came upon the raging Jordan River. Joshua knew that he was walking in the will of God, on a mission to fulfill his purpose. When he stepped into those torrential waters with the people following him, Joshua fully expected God would provide.

This is how I live my life. I know that I am living out my purpose. I don't always know what is next, but I do know that I have to do my part and keep moving purposefully forward. I trust that the answers and provisions will come. So far, they have and I can't wait to see what is next! :)

PART ONE
The Chicktime Story

Chapter 1

Why Chicktime?

The tragedy of life is in what dies inside a man while he lives – the death of genuine feeling, the death of inspired response, the awareness that makes it possible to feel the pain or the glory of other men in yourself.

– Norman Cousins

It wasn't long after Chicktime got rolling that I began to see the impact. Not just in my life, but in the lives of all the volunteers who shared those early days. Our lives dramatically changed. All of our lives. There is something about being in the presence of severely abused, neglected, lost and lonely children that wakes you up. Makes you realize how precious life is, and how important it is to be your best.

When we are around the children we serve, we are at our best because we know they deserve it. They deserve our undivided attention. We leave our cell phones in the car and focus on their words rather than forming our next sentences. They deserve mercy, so we give them as much as they can soak up, our eyes communicating things to children that no words could match.

I've seen it a thousand times. A softness settles over the volunteers. The harsh realities of our daily lives and struggles vanish as we come into the presence of these wounded children, and become absorbed in their need for our attention. It is holy ground. When you walk in that realm, it stays with you long after the goodbyes and the closing of many doors and gates. As we drive away, enveloped by the soft whir of air conditioning, we cry over lost innocence. Or, giggle over the childlike connections we made that day. And every time we think about our own lives, and of how much we have, we begin to process how we can do something to make life better for others.

This is the dramatic change wrought by Chicktime. The organization puts you on the path to figuring out how you can help improve the lives of others. Oftentimes, this sense of purpose translates into a deeper relationship with the charity the local Chicktime chapter serves. And sometimes, Chicktime simply helps you see where you need to move next – and it may have absolutely NOTHING to do with your local Chicktime chapter.

Let me share a few examples. The first Chicktime chapter formed in late 2006. We had our first official Chicktime event in January 2007 at a local residential treatment center for severely abused little girls. Within a very short amount of time, our volunteers assumed enormous responsibility. They joined the board of the children's center, began volunteering in various programs the center offered, and advocated in the community for financial support for the center. Some even quit their jobs and went to work full time for the children's center. Others stayed involved with Chicktime for a season, but then moved deeper into their life's purpose down the avenues they began to see.

I know their time with the children helped determine where they would ultimately serve. They've all shared their stories with me. I smile because I see their faces even as I write. It is such a joy to see women using their gifts to impact the world ... and I'm happy I am able to be a part of their story!

About a year into our first chapter, another phenomenon emerged. Women who volunteered with us began to take action in the political realm. Women are strong and are passionate about injustice. I would hear stories of this volunteer or that getting involved with CASA, making calls to their representatives in Congress, joining boards for organizations fighting injustice, traveling to Washington D.C. to advocate on Capitol Hill, and simply bringing the issue of abuse out of the dark and into the forefront of their conversations. For you see, child abuse is a daunting issue with so few solutions that women tend to shy away from even talking about it. We're passionate about expressing our disgust for those who abuse, and even attack the system for not getting a handle on the problem.

Chicktime changes all that. Our group somehow births courage in women. I don't know how it happens but I'm glad it does. I like to reflect on a phrase by Richard Sterns, the president of World Vision, the largest humanitarian-relief organization in the world (not the Red Cross, bigger!). He places starving African children in perspective by making them part of our homes, a force to be reckoned with in our daily lives. He suggests as we wake up, get ready for our day, head out the door with our briefcase, tote bag, or backpack strapped on and a cup coffee or water bottle in hand and open the front door... we suddenly see a child laying on our welcome mat. He is tiny, almost skeletal. His tummy is bloated from the effects of ravaging hunger. He is quietly weeping. He looks up with soft round eyes, and we stop in our hurried tracks, late for wherever it is we are going. We have a decision to make. We can step over him and go about our day, or put down our stuff and pick him up, rush him to the hospital, and get him the medical attention he needs.

Spending time with children of abuse is much the same. Once a woman becomes intimately acquainted with those soft round eyes, she has a decision to make. Continue about her daily life, or do something. Abuse becomes personal. We begin to explore ways we can help rather than sit by and feel helpless.

The cycle of abuse is ugly. Sadly, many children of abuse grow up and repeat the cycle by abusing their own children. Not all certainly, but too many eventually become abusers. What would happen if someone stepped in and showed them love? What if they felt valued and empowered to live a life of purpose? Think about the investment of time we make in our own children. The daily hugs, the I love you's, the meals cooked and carpools driven. The hours we sit on the sidelines of their lives cheering them on. Most children of abuse have NO idea what that is like. They are alone for the most part, spending much of their time avoiding their abusers as an act of self-preservation.

When they are rescued, taken from their homes and placed in shelters, centers or even with foster families, just think of the GIGANTIC hole in their hearts that causes children of abuse to wonder day-in and day-out if they are worthy. If they truly matter ... if they have value? The local community MUST rally around these children and answer these questions for them. We must go to them. Spend time with them. Invest in them. Tell them they are special. Tell them how much we enjoy spending time with them. They need to hear our laughter as we respond to their silly stories. They need to hear the warmth of our voice when they share their dreams. They just need us. Period. Not all of us all of the time, just a regular shot in the arm from the local community making these children a priority.

I would like to end this chapter with a story. It is a piece of inspirational fiction written by John W. Schlatter. When I first read this little story almost two decades ago, it re-shaped my life. I hope it helps shape yours as you explore the possibilities of living a life of love, regularly reaching out to those around you.

WRITES SCHLATTER: One day, when I was a freshman in high school, I saw a kid from my class was walking home from school. His name was Kyle. It looked like he was carrying all of his books. I thought to myself, "Why would anyone bring home all his books on a Friday? He must really be a nerd." I had quite a weekend planned (parties and a football game with my friends tomorrow afternoon), so I shrugged my shoulders and went on. As I was walking, I saw a bunch of kids running toward him. They ran at him, knocking all his books out of his arms and tripping him so he landed in the dirt. His glasses went flying, and I saw them land in the grass about 10 feet from him. He looked up and I saw this terrible sadness in his eyes. My heart went out to him. So, I jogged over to him as he crawled around looking for his glasses, and I saw a tear in his eye. As I handed him his glasses, I said, 'Those guys are jerks. They really should get lives.'

He looked at me and said, 'Hey thanks!' There was a big smile on his face. It was one of those smiles that showed real gratitude. I helped him pick up his books, and asked him where he lived. As it turned out, he lived near me, so I asked him why I had never seen him before. He said he had gone to private school before now. I would have never hung out with a private school kid before. We talked all the way home, and I carried some of his books. He turned out to be a pretty cool kid. I asked him if he wanted to play a little football with my friends. He said 'yes.' We hung out all weekend and the more I got to know Kyle, the more I liked him, and my friends thought the same of him. Monday morning came, and there was Kyle with the huge stack of books again. I stopped him and said, 'Boy, you are gonna really build some serious muscles with this pile of books everyday!' He just laughed and handed me half the books.

Over the next four years, Kyle and I became best friends. When we were seniors we began to think about college. Kyle decided on Georgetown and I was going to Duke. I knew that we would always be friends, that the miles would never be a problem. He was going to be a doctor and I was going for business on a football scholarship. Kyle was valedictorian of our class. I teased him all the time about being a nerd. He had to prepare a speech for graduation. I was so glad it wasn't me having to get up there and speak.

Graduation day, I saw Kyle. He looked great. He was one of those guys that really found himself during high school. He filled out and actually looked good in glasses. He had more dates than I had and all the girls loved him. Boy, sometimes I was jealous! Today was one of those days. I could see that he was nervous about his speech. So, I smacked him on the back and said, 'Hey, big guy, you'll be great!' He looked at me with one of those looks (the really grateful one) and smiled. 'Thanks,' he said.

As he started his speech, he cleared his throat, and began 'Graduation is a time to thank those who helped you make it through those tough years. Your parents, your teachers, your siblings, maybe a coach ... but mostly your friends ... I am here to tell all of you that being a friend to someone is the best gift you can give them. I am going to tell you a story.' I just looked at my friend with disbelief as he told the story of the first day we met. He had planned to kill himself over the weekend. He talked of how he had cleaned out his locker so his mom wouldn't have to do it later and was carrying his stuff home. He looked hard at me and gave me a little smile. 'Thankfully, I was saved. My friend saved me from doing the unspeakable.' I heard the gasp go through the crowd as this handsome, popular boy told us all about his weakest moment. I saw his mom and Dad looking at me and smiling that same grateful smile. Not until that moment did I realize its depth.

Never underestimate the power of your actions. With one small gesture you can change a person's life. For better or for worse. God puts us all in each other's lives to impact one another in some way.

Chapter 2

The Story

One word frees us of all the weight and pain of life:
that word is love.

– Sophocles

Everyone has a beginning and a story. So does every organization. The Chicktime story born in my heart beats today in the hearts of many other women across America. The story of how Chicktime originally began is no more important than the story of how each chapter begins… for you see… each chapter is born in the heart of its founder… just as the original chapter and the Chicktime organization began in mine. You can read and enjoy every story online at Chicktime.com by clicking on the chapters and reading about them. These are my favorite stories of all. I read and re-read them all the time.

Because so many people ask me how Chicktime began, I will tell you the story here. But please, know that you are only seeing the tip of the iceberg as you read about my encounter with destiny … every chapter's beginning will take your breath away with the depth of passion and purpose that brought each chapter founder to embark on her journey.

Chicktime happened because of my daughter, Katy. She was 15-years-old at the time. I had dreamed of being a mother my entire life. I knew it would be my life's work. My mom became very ill when I was just a little girl. She ended up becoming very depressed because of her illness and just kind of gave up on life. She hung on and existed until I was in my mid-twenties, and then something remarkable happened. She stopped focusing on what little health she did have and celebrated what she had left. By this time, she was completely bed-ridden, riddled and ravaged by the effects of multiple sclerosis. She could only communicate by blinking her eyes... but I was able to enjoy almost six years with a really cool mom... and I'm glad it ended well. Unfortunately, that doesn't change the fact that as a child, she wasn't able to really parent me. I was alone as a child. My dad did what he could but he was busy trying to deal with my mom and that left little for me. My childhood dramatically shaped the kind of mother I would be. Sometimes good, sometimes bad... I guess it is the same with all of us.

Anyway, when Katy turned 15, it was obvious that in spite of my lofty intentions of being a great mom, something wasn't going well. She didn't particularly like me, and she really didn't seem to have much value for anything I had to say. Rather than get mad, I decided to reach her in the only way I knew how – through other women. She listened to them. And so I told her one Friday morning before school that she would be spending the weekend with me at a women's conference. You can imagine her joy!

It was during that conference that a life was changed dramatically. Mine.

Katy really enjoyed the speakers, my girlfriends were there (whom she adored) and it was a wonderful weekend.

AS A SIDE NOTE: After I began sharing this experience with other women, I quickly learned that most every mother of a teenage daughter experiences what I did with Katy (at one time or another) and it is completely normal for a teenage daughter to not adore her mom all of the time! But remember, I didn't have a mom well enough to teach me these things!

Back to the conference! One of the speakers really impacted me. She talked of the pain in the world. I was aware of pain. I had experienced my fair share! But she went deeper. She began talking about other people's pain and how we have a responsibility to do something to ease theirs. Well, I could identify with that, too. I was there for my children and husband when they were hurting. I volunteered at my children's school, tutoring at-risk kids, supporting Little League, working with Girl Scouts, and all kinds of other organizations that helped others. But the speaker went deeper. She talked about the kind of pain that I had no framework for. Pain unrelated to me, my life, my children, my family or my friends.

She told the story of friend whose daughter served as a missionary in Africa. She told of how her friend just couldn't wrap her mind around her daughter's dedication to these horrifically pained people. A people who lost their children to the LRA, child-slavery, death through starvation, malaria, AIDS, etc. The mother asked her daughter, "How do you do it? How do you wake up every day and face this kind of pain? Day after day?" And the daughter looked at her mother and said the words that changed the course of my life forever, "But mom, whether I see the pain or not, it still exists."

I thought of those mothers, eternally helpless in their mud-floored huts holding onto their starving children with nothing to offer them to eat except the mud they slept on. Or the mothers who had to watch their children murder their own fathers because the LRA had come in the middle of the night and held guns to their mom's head and would pull the trigger if the child did not kill their father. Or of the mothers alone in their villages at night crying for their children, whereabouts unknown because the child was stolen by sex traders. This is the pain the speaker was referring to.

I sat in my chair stunned. I had volunteered all of my life, but never in a way that ushered in hope to an almost hopelessly broken soul. And I made a decision. I was going to find the pain in the world and do something about it. Katy and I talked and she was in, too.

We realized that we needed to target a population that we had a heart for. Life has taught me it is imperative that a woman be passionate about the group she serves in order to truly map out her life's purpose. Because we were doing this together, I first deferred to what Katy is passionate about. She loves animals so we discussed the possibility of becoming involved with the local animal shelter. It would have been great for her, but I barely even like cats.

After much discussion, we landed on a children's center only 15 minutes from our house. We had passed by many, many times but had avoided it because we were told it was for bad kids. Kids who were going to prison if they didn't shape up. It was a residential treatment center for youths with addictions to drugs, alcohol and many other deep issues. At first, they wouldn't let us volunteer directly with the girls because Katy was too young. Their regulations required volunteers working directly with the kids to be 21 years or older. So Katy and I shopped, purchasing items the children's center could stock in its behavior-point store. We filled it with things any teenage girl would love: Lotions, sweet-smelling soaps, lip glosses, decorative pillows, fun slippers, bracelets, games, craft supplies, etc.

We also learned that most of the children at the center were abused and/or neglected, with 95 percent them victims of sexual abuse. We learned that yes, the girls did have addiction problems, but they developed them as coping mechanisms to deal with the traumas they endured from a very young age. We learned that some of their drug-addicted parents often hooked their own children on drugs as a way to coerce them to party with the drug dealers...others offering their own children for sexual favors in return for the drugs. We learned many of the girls cut themselves as a way to deal with their emotional suffering. Pain from the physical wounds distracted their minds from the memories they so desperately wanted to forget. We became more dedicated than ever, and determined to stay involved.

After about eight weeks, we were invited to attend the annual Christmas party with the girls. Finally, we were going to be able to spend TIME with them. The day of the party came, and what we experienced propelled me to kick into high gear and figure out a way to regularly bring the women of the local community into the presence of these children. During the party, I discovered these children were JUST LIKE my own daughter. They looked the same, had the same mannerisms and catch phrases, yet they were in DESPERATE need of attention. They longed to have visitors and yearned for connection with others. I thought of the many remarkable women in my life, so filled with talents and passions. I thought about the wonderful opportunities we could collectively provide to the girls by teaching them things their own mothers were unable to expose them to. Normal activities like art, dance, gardening, cooking, sewing, budgeting, yoga, sports and so much more. I thought of my own life and how in the past eight weeks I had all but forgotten about my own problems. Instead, I was focusing on the positive things about my life, my strengths and ideas about how I could help these girls even more. And I realized … not only do these children need my friends, my friends need them, too!!!

And so Chicktime began. The Christmas party took place in early December, and somehow between that time and the second week in January, I developed a comprehensive program, obtained approval from the center, convinced my friends to get on board ... and we had our very first Chicktime event! Now, only a few years later, on any given Saturday, there are Chicktime events happening simultaneously throughout our country in children's homes/centers/shelters.

Through these gatherings, women enter the presence of these almost-forgotten children. Lives are changing. I do believe we will see a shift in the issue of abuse in my lifetime. I pray daily for all abuse to end, and I do my part to help victims realize there is a better way ... that they deserve much, much more and in fact have the capacity to discover who they were meant to be and with love, become that person. My greatest joy is seeing the grown up victims of child abuse join Chicktime as adults, going back into the homes/centers/shelters they once called home to love on and bring hope to the next generation.

Chapter 3

The Growth

I don't know what your destiny will be, but one thing I know: the only ones among you who will be really happy are those who have sought and found how to serve.

– Albert Schweitzer

I believe in human dignity as the source of national purpose, human liberty as the source of national action, the human heart as the source of national compassion, and the human mind as the source of our invention and our ideas.

– John Fitzgerald Kennedy

The most important and possibly the ONLY thing you need from this chapter is an understanding of how Chicktime grows. Let me begin with how we DON'T grow.

Chicktime doesn't recruit new leaders. Ever. Chicktime doesn't pay our leaders. Ever. Chicktime doesn't ask our leader to 'pay it forward' and commit to helping other women start 'X' number of chapters. Ever.

Chicktime grows when the yearning in woman's heart meets our mission.

The Internet plays a big role. When a woman Googles 'volunteer opportunities,' somehow Chicktime shows up in her search. And as she reads about us, something stirs her heart to get involved. She contacts us, and if she is really ready to rally the women in her community, the next chapter begins. It is that simple.

Even with rapid growth, our chapters all function basically the same. We have a strategic and proven model. Each Chicktime chapter follows the basic Chicktime model, and each new chapter-founder trains personally with Chicktime's national founder. Me. I feel moved to personally impart the vision to new chapters. I have very passionate friends who help move new chapters through the training process. From there, the founders train their co-leaders and even subsequent chapter leaders. Established chapter leaders also play a role in training new chapter leaders in surrounding communities. They host new leaders for Chicktime events. There is no better way to catch the vision than by simply experiencing Chicktime. So new leaders reach out to established chapter leaders and ask to attend a Chicktime event and soak up their knowledge.

Many people wonder how an organization can grow as quickly and as successfully as Chicktime yet still maintain the integrity of the mission and vision. The answer is twofold and simple. First, we have an effective, proven model that is easy to implement. Easy equals fun and Chicktime is fun! Second, we are a decentralized organization that values the passion of the local leader. We recognize that the best knowledge is at the 'fringe' of any organization. Those closest to the population they directly serve, and the volunteers they directly lead, have the best knowledge to tackle the unique challenges that come up. Local leaders are not micromanaged. The passion of the local leader fuels her to establish her chapter based on her vision, and grow her local chapter to make an impact in her local community. Women don't like being told what to do. They have dreams and sometimes just need help with the practical stuff. When a woman's dream aligns with the vision of Chicktime, we provide the tools to help turn her dream into reality.

Chapter 4

The Chicktime Model

Don't ask yourself what the world needs; ask yourself what makes you come alive. And then go and do that. Because what the world needs are people who have come alive.

– Howard Thurman

Without passion man is a mere latent force and possibility, like the flint which awaits the shock of the iron before it can give forth its spark."

– Henri Frederic Amiel

The Chicktime Model is based on everything I love about volunteering – and nothing that I don't like! After almost 20 years of volunteering with various organizations, I was able to observe what worked and what didn't. I observed what drew volunteers to the organizations they served, and the reasons so many eventually stopped coming.

I am keenly aware that we are each given a few obvious talents. I can't dance, I certainly can't sing, I'm really bad at math, and could name a hundred things I really stink at. But I do have an unusual talent. I am a strategist. Most people who know me see very quickly that my mind observes everything going on around me and I reorganize the pieces to make everything flow better. This quality can be highly annoying (just ask my family). I'm learning to turn it off when it is unappreciated so that I don't drive everyone around me nuts! To many people, I can appear just plain bossy ... and to be honest ... that is a quality I possess and I constantly fight. There isn't a doubt in my mind that I fight an evil 'twin.' I think we all do to some degree ... the characteristics just change from person to person based on their strengths.

Back to the Chicktime Model!

This model was developed in a very short period of time. It was as if the pieces I'd collected over the course of my lifetime all tumbled out on a yellow pad in a two-hour span. I wrote it all down, typed it up and then went down to the children's center where I volunteered and asked them if we could try it out. They agreed, and the rest is history. As technology changes, our tools develop and change, but the basic model is still the same.

Each Chicktime chapter partners with a local charity. A typical Chicktime chapter consists of three core leaders, 12 monthly workshop/activity leaders (a different woman each month, based on the Bunco concept!), and lots of members. Most chapters grow to 100-plus members! What do the volunteers do who aren't leading the workshop/activity that month? They show up and play!! Each monthly activity/workshop leader identifies her gift – something she loves to do – and turns it into an activity appropriate for the children (or whatever population) the chapter serves. There is so much passion and joy wrapped up in the activity/workshop that everyone present can't help but wonder, "what is my passion… and how can I use it to bring joy to others?" If you are not the leader that month, as a volunteer, you just show up to assist the leader and play with the children (or whatever population) your charity serves – guilt-free serving!

The idea is to expose the next generation to a wide array of gifts and talents so they can look inside themselves to identify their own.

Chicktime exists as a vehicle for bringing women in the local community into the presence of children (and/or women) healing from abuse and neglect. It is our hope that the local Chicktime chapter develops into a robust community open to all women interested in giving back and making a difference in the lives of others. It is also our hope to have a network of Chicktime chapters throughout the United States so that women can plug in and serve no matter where they move, visit, work or play.

Chicktime is a no-guilt organization that capitalizes on the strengths of its members and leaders. We encourage women to come when they can, to lead a monthly workshop/activity when they are ready, but also to completely accept there is only so much any woman can do. It serves no purpose to add another burden on already overtaxed lives. We fully believe that Chicktime will give back more to the volunteer than it will take... and it is this sole reason that we believe every woman should try it out. At least once.

There are many incredible organizations throughout the country that serve victims of abuse. They need our help. Chicktime partners with these local groups to bring workshops/activities to the victims they serve. For the most part, it truly takes a village to raise these children to become healthy, whole and happy adults. The adult victims we serve also need the community to rally around them and help them discover their value. For when people acknowledge their own self-worth, they rise up and become filled with passion. These formerly abused women recognize their own unique gifts, and learn to use them to help others.

There is so much pain in our nation. Many of us ache with a sense of helplessness when it comes to salving the wounds of victims of abuse. When we hear the stories of abuse played out in our own communities, usually after the fact, we feel anger ... and desperately seek a quick-and-effective way to jump in NOW and do something. That is what these children need, someone to jump in NOW and do something. This is where Chicktime comes in. Rather than lament that you don't know what to do, go online, sign up to receive invitations from your local Chicktime chapter (or start one if needed), and seek out organizations that serve the victims of abuse in your area. Every Chicktime chapter partners with one, so that is a great place to start! There are fabulous organizations out there already tackling the heart of this issue – they just need more support to do what they do so their reach is longer and the healing salve is more abundant.

Why Chicktime? Most organizations that serve victims of abuse don't have an easy way for new volunteers to credibly plug in and volunteer without a long-term commitment or extensive training. Chicktime is a great way to get started. For some, Chicktime is a starting place. Many volunteers will eventually go back and get more deeply involved with the organization, volunteering to serve on their boards, working as mentors and supporting fundraising events ... they become advocates for the local charity. Others become well-acquainted with the faces and the real people behind this issue of abuse and begin to acquaint themselves with laws before Congress that will better protect the victims... they become political advocates. And for all, Chicktime induces intro- spection. Volunteers begin asking themselves the important ques- tions: "What are my unique gifts? Am I using them to invest in the lives of others? Am I living my life in a way that my children and grandchildren will know that I stood for something im- portant?"

So, do you need Chicktime to volunteer with victims of abuse? Of course not. That would be ridiculous. Chicktime is meant to help you get OTHER women involved. Women who are graceful, talented, gifted, kind and filled with passion ... but may- be never even thought there was a way for them to make a differ- ence in the issue of abuse. There is a way, and if Chicktime isn't already in your community, you might be just the one to bring it!

Part 2
How-To Guide

Chapter 5

Establishing and Leading a Chapter

First of all, let me apologize for not sharing this information on a more personal level. This chapter is the motivation for writing this book. With so many requests coming in every day for new chapter startups, I was overwhelmed. Up until after midnight most nights, I transitioned out of my job. My kids were feeling the strain, and my dear husband was so patient ... for he knows the impact Chicktime is making in the lives of the women who lead and volunteer ... and the victims that we are dedicated to find and support! It was taking most of my life just to return all of the emails ... and so I reluctantly decided to write this operating manual to fully reach every woman whose heart is yearning to make a difference ... while maintaining my own equilibrium.

With that said, I hope you enjoy reading through my thoughts on the responsibilities of chapter leadership. I started the very first Chicktime chapter in 2006, and since that time, hundreds of women have trained using our model. There truly is a basic pattern, and it really is a simple one.

If you are thinking about establishing a chapter, read through this book. Once you've made a commitment to move forward and startup/lead a chapter in your area, find a charity with a residential population serving victims of abuse/neglect. Most counties had a children's shelter or shelter for victims of domestic violence. Homeless shelters can also work if more specialized shelters in your area do not exist.

Before we begin your training, you will need to do a few things. First, read through the Leader Resources section of the Chicktime.com website. Also, finishing this book is really important, as it will allow our trainings to focus on you, rather than reviewing the Chicktime Model and responsibilities of the leader. Finishing this book will also allow you time to ponder if starting a Chicktime chapter is right for you at this season in your life. Lastly and perhaps most importantly, find a charity in your area with a residential population caring for victims of abuse/neglect and begin volunteering there. It is critical that you find a charity you love and have formed a personal relationship with before we can formally begin your training. If you would like help finding one or just want to talk with us, please reach out to info@chicktime.com, and a volunteer will help you. We are here for you. We are a sisterhood. No one needs to ever feel alone in their quest to make a read difference in our world!

Setting up a Chicktime chapter isn't hard, but it does take a solid commitment and definitely a heart to bring women alongside you... to help them WAKE UP to the need ... and to get busy!! You certainly don't need Chicktime to volunteer with abused children... we are here to help you get OTHER women to volunteer! And you will have a ball, Chicktime is a ton of fun and ohhhh so rewarding. Especially when the women you bring with you to serve are a bit depressed and not feeling great about their own lives ... they will begin to blossom as they volunteer with you, and you will have peace knowing that you helped your friends ... along with the satisfaction of knowing you helped bring hope and comfort to the abused/neglected children you will serve.

We should probably start with what you will actually do as a chapter leader. This is a lot of information and will be covered in detail should you decide to continue and set up the chapter ... but I want you to make sure you know what you are getting into!

Chapter set up starts and ends with personal trainings. It usually takes about three hour-long training sessions to take the vision for your chapter out of your mind/heart and translate that vision into an established relationship with a children's home, shelter, or organization in your local area that serves victims of abuse/neglect. Most training sessions are conducted over the phone. You will also receive Web coaching to walk you through using our online tools.

The trainings are deeply personal and tailored for each individual leader so I won't be able to go into much detail about that here. You (the new leader) determine the pace ... some leaders are so excited they cram all of their trainings into six weeks and they are off and running with volunteer events on their calendars and a fire under them that only God could light. It is with these leaders that I have learned to step back and soak it all in ... they are walking on holy ground and I've decided not to get in the way by being the voice of reason. For most women though, and with my strong recommendation, the chapter startup process takes between eight to 12 weeks ... although ... we have some leaders on the four-month plan ... which is fine with me ... again ... we move at YOUR pace.

Chicktime truly is a no-guilt organization, and we honor every leader for moving at a pace that is comfortable for her. We do ask that you commit to completing your training within a four-month window or wait until you can commit to that goal before contacting us to get started.

Getting Started

So here we go: From a practical standpoint, it will take you about eight to 12 weeks to get a chapter going, typically about an hour a week. The training will formally begin AFTER you have built a personal relationship with a local charity with a residential population caring for victims of abuse/neglect. Once the training begins, we will share next steps and homework after each training call. Most leaders complete the training in 3-5 training calls and follow-up homework assignments.

There is no charge to you for the training, and we volunteer our time to train you. Our goal for the training is to help you organize a local chapter in your area following the Chicktime model, coach you to recruit a strong team, and ensure you identify a rising managing leader should you ever move out of the area or need to step out of leadership in the future. Building a Chicktime Network is our vision, and we are so happy you have chosen to join us and bring Chicktime to your area so that other women can plug in their passions and make a real difference in the lives of others.

Ongoing Responsibilities

After the organization of the chapter is complete, you as the leader will have ongoing responsibilities. Timeframe: you will typically spend about four hours a month on Chicktime. You'll need to budget about two hours on the phone and the computer or iPad, updating your Chicktime web page, sending out invitations to the monthly Chicktime event, and coordinating with your volunteer workshop/activity leader that month to make sure all is well. In addition, leadership also requires coordinating the event with your charity partner. You also will spend about two hours a month with the children/victims, actually enjoying the Chicktime activity. It is honestly a VERY easy group to lead!

Committed Workshop/Activity Leaders

Your main role as chapter leader is to get commitments from women in your area to lead one of the monthly activities at your children's home. You will lead the first one, but most likely that is the only Chicktime event you will actually organize and facilitate in each calendar year. Your friends and colleagues will each take a turn leading the rest of the monthly activities.

I recommend a simple activity based on something you love to do. You will want a very good friend to lead the second month. Let's say she loves to scrapbook, so she gathers a couple of her scrapbooking friends, all of the materials, organizes the activity and then leads the second Chicktime event at the children's home. Then let's say you have invited the cook from your favorite restaurant to come out and teach the kids a cooking class for the third Chicktime. So that cook will gather any helpers he/she needs, all of the ingredients, pots, pans, etc, and will organize the cooking class schedule.

You see, if you do your job well, you won't come up with activities, you will simply make sure to have your months filled with leaders who love what they are going to teach the kids.

The possibilities are endless: A girlfriend who loves manicures organizes a manicure Chicktime-event, a friend who loves yoga (may or may not be a certified instructor, doesn't matter) comes out and teaches a yoga class for the month she has signed up to lead, a friend who thinks everyone should know how to change a tire and oil in the car comes out and teaches that for her workshop. Are you getting the picture? Your goal is to BRING the women from your community into the presence of these children so they can share their love and passion for their hobbies and vocations. When they do, something extraordinary happens. The children we serve and the volunteers who showed up that day will feel the joy of the leader and realize they too can tap into their own unique qualities that they love, and use them to help others! This is why we NEVER want to just sit around and try to figure out what the kids would like to do and then organize something based on what we think they would enjoy. NO ... you want to engage women in your local community and invite them to turn their hobby or vocation into an activity the children will enjoy. And that makes all the difference.

Let's go a little deeper. As you begin recruiting monthly workshop/activity leaders you will learn to have conversations that go like this:

YOU: "Hi Jill, I'm so glad that you are excited about Chicktime!"

JILL: "Yeah, I feel so lucky to have so much love in my life and I want to do what I can to help the kids. Thank you for setting all this up so I can come out and volunteer with them. Let me know if there is anything you need."

YOU: "Well, funny you ask. We need two more workshop/activity leaders this year to fill up our schedule. The kids love knowing in advance that we have committed leaders, and it really helps everyone plan when we know we have someone we can depend on commit to lead a workshop. You seem perfect. Would you like to lead a workshop? We have August and October open."

JILL: "Me? Really? I would love to but I'm a bit scared, I don't know what I would do with them. What do they like to do?"

You: "Gosh, they like to do just about anything. What do YOU love to do? What are your hobbies, what do you like to do when you have extra time? What makes you happy?"

JILL: "I love to read but I don't know how that could be an activity for the kids."

YOU: "How about this, do you have a favorite book from when you were young? If so, you could set up an author's workshop. You could read a chapter or two from the book, get the kids really into it and then pull out a stack of journals. The kids could then take one if they wanted to and begin writing their own stories. You could write a page of yours (in advance) and read it to them to help get them started. It could be fiction or non-fiction. Another neat idea would be to bring copies of the book that you read and let them take copies with them to finish the story on their own."

JILL: "Wow, I would have never thought of that. I would love to. I saw composition books at the Dollar Store for one-dollar each. And I could order gently used copies of the book from Amazon.com, I bet I could get them for less than $1 a copy. How many kids typically come?"

YOU: "Those are great ideas. We typically have 15 to 25 kids. It would be best to plan for 25. Do you have the money in your budget for the notebooks and copies of the paperback?"

JILL: "I have some, but not enough. My boss is very supportive of community service and I would be comfortable asking him to donate up to $50. If he can't do that much, I can ask a few friends to pitch in. My book club would probably LOVE to help, and my best girlfriends would help, too. We typically meet at Starbucks once a month to catch up, and I can invite them to my house for coffee instead and ask them to donate the money they would have spent on the coffee to my book fund. Gosh, I have five months before my turn to lead, so it shouldn't be a problem getting the supplies together before then. HEY, can I serve a snack? It would be fun to have hot tea or at least bottled water and a cookie."

YOU: "You are going to have so much fun with this, and the kids are going to LOVE it. I can't wait, either. I would like a copy of the book, too. If you really do find them for less than a dollar, count me in for one! And yes, refreshments are always appreciated!"

YOU: "Also, you will need to bring along a few volunteers you know you can count on to help facilitate your activity. Would someone from the book club you mentioned by interested?"

JILL: "Oh my gosh, YES! My friend Susie loves to write short stories and I could bring her to help with the journals and give a quick lesson on writing their own stories. She adores kids and I've already told her about Chicktime!"

YOU: "Perfect. So, would you prefer August or October?"

JILL: "October. That will give me more time!"

YOU: "Okay, you can check out our monthly workshop/activity leader guidelines posted on our website, and I will contact you about six weeks before and touch base on the details. Thank you so much!!"

You will have SO much fun with these conversations. Begin practicing them on your family and friends so you will be prepared when the time comes. It may be in the grocery store line with a complete stranger or the dinner table with a dear friend. Get prepared!!

Roles

From a practical standpoint, let's dive into what a typical month looks like for you, the chapter leader.

Every month, you will contact the upcoming workshop/activity leader, make sure she has the date on her calendar, make sure she understands her responsibilities as the leader (such as bringing all of the materials and helpers she needs to facilitate her workshop/event), and also find out what she is planning for her event. Then you will offer to make an invitation that you will email out to the women on your chapter roster. Online registration is available and makes life so much easier!!! This step (making contact with the workshop/activity leader) is critical and without it ... your chapter will never work. To make your life easier, I have created a 'monthly leader' guideline page on the Chicktime.com website under *Member Resources*. This is meant to help your monthly workshop/activity leaders understand the general expectations of someone who agrees to lead a monthly activity. I highly encourage each chapter leader to customize this set of guidelines for her chapter and post it on her Chicktime.com web page. You can find a sample on the Chicktime TX- Canyon Lake web page titled *How We Serve.*

To share a bit about what happens WHILE you are facilitating a Chicktime event: You and the non-leading volunteers show up and play. The monthly leader brings her own helpers so neither you NOR the other volunteers most likely help facilitate the activity. You and the non-leading volunteers are going to have the most fun (but the monthly leader will get the most out of it ... we can talk about that during training ... ask me about it). Basically, the volunteers who just show up and play do just that!!! They get to participate in these yoga sessions, cooking classes, scrapbooking, etc. as participants who just play along with the kids ... if the kids are on the yoga mats doing yoga, then so are the volunteers who just showed up to play ... if the kids are chopping onions during the cooking class, so are the volunteers ... it is just so much fun to BE with the kids and do what they do as an active participant ... it truly communicates that you WANT to be with them as you assimilate into their lives during the activity! The giggles and the hugs are so memorable ... your volunteers will NEVER forget the experiences they will have during Chicktime events.

SPECIAL NOTE: It is EXTREMELY important that you OR one of your core chapter co-leaders (I recommend that every chapter have three core chapter co-leaders) is present at EVERY single Chicktime event. Your monthly workshop/activity leader is most likely NEW to the home. They won't know where to go to set up, they won't feel comfortable welcoming the volunteers, they won't have time to ensure everyone has the opportunity to get a Chicktime T-shirt, and they won't know the staff members. These are all of the little things that a good host needs to do to make an event successful. These are the JOBS of the chapter leader or co-leader!! So make sure to recruit two other women to co-lead the chapter with you so that when you can't make it to a Chicktime event, someone you trust who knows the ropes will be there to act as host!!

Finding a Charity Partner

If all of this still sounds like something you want to do ... to get the ball rolling ... if you haven't already identified a children's home/shelter/organization in your area, I would recommend you Google that and narrow your search down to an organization closer to your ZIP code. It is extremely important for you to identify the age group/population you are drawn to serve. When you begin your search, if you have an idea of WHO you are drawn to serve, your search will be more productive. You will find there are organizations that serve children, specialize in teens, or treat children with severe emotional trauma related to abuse (these are typically called RTCs or Residential Treatment Centers). You will find homes for runaways, young pregnant mothers, the homeless, shelters for victims of domestic abuse, and of course homes for the elderly. I have found that women are moved to serve specific age groups/populations, and since YOU are the chapter founder, YOU get to decide which group your chapter will serve.

Once you find a charity you are drawn to, contact them as an individual – not as Chicktime – and plug in as a volunteer. Once you volunteer there two or three times, you will have a good idea whether the charity is a good match for you personally. This is imperative. We cannot emphasize strongly enough the step of building your personal relationship with a local charity is critical and must happen before we can begin your training.

Making the Commitment

Well ... there you go ... a detailed overview of what to expect if you decide to lead your local chapter. From personal experience, I can tell you that leading women in your community into the presence of abused/neglected children is one of the most powerful and effective ways to raise awareness and open hearts to this issue ... hearts that closed long ago because it was just too painful ... and minds that shut to this issue because of the helpless feeling that overwhelms us. The problem is just so big ... that it keeps most women from moving into action. But YOU, my sweet sister, have a tool at your disposal to make a difference. Yes, it does take some work to start up and lead a chapter, but someone has to do it. Most communities have NOT one vehicle that allows busy women from the local community to come into the presence of children healing from abuse/neglect. Chicktime makes a place for everyone (no matter how busy they are). Most volunteer opportunities in these facilities (if they even offer volunteer opportunities) require a huge commitment. Sadly, that disqualifies most women because they don't have time. Chicktime is different because we understand women are busy. Our model accommodates this. The Chicktime structure allows everyone to do something. And when everyone does something ... the world becomes a better place.

NOTE: You must be 21 years or older to lead a Chicktime chapter. If you aren't 21, I can help you find a place to serve now and when you are old enough ... we can start the chapter then. I invest in leaders and leaders invest in their chapters. I am happy to invest in you even if it takes several years for you to reach 21!

Chapter 6

The Chicktime Tools

To really grasp the breadth of the Chicktime tools, you need to visit the chicktime.com website. All of our most current tools are online listed under *Leader Resources*.

Because technology is rapidly moving forward, and Chicktime is moving with it, it would be pointless to list the detailed information pertaining to the tools here on the printed page. Rather than go into great detail, let me just say that I have dedicated my life to researching and providing local chapter leaders with great tools to help run their chapters. Because I lead my own chapter, I have a working knowledge of the tools needed and I regularly update our offerings.

Chicktime.com lists the tools and provides the latest training tutorials for each tool.

Most of the Chicktime tools are available free-of-charge to chapter leaders. Some include:

- ❖ Chicktime.com, unlimited web pages
- ❖ Online calendar listings at chicktime.com and volunteermatch.org
- ❖ Online registration for local chapter Chicktime events
- ❖ Chicktime volunteer management software
- ❖ Chicktime Branded Social Media Page
- ❖ Chicktime leadership training

For more detailed information: visit chicktime.com and click on Leader Resources.

Chapter 7

Co-Leaders and Letting Go

Chapter co-leaders will be a critical component to your chapter. If you think you can do this alone and don't need them, let me assure you, you are mistaken. Your co-leaders will be key to filling in the blanks. For example, most founding chapter leaders are quite outgoing and charismatic. But they often lack administration or computer skills. Oftentimes they aren't good with budgeting. And almost certainly the local chapter leader will not be able to attend every single chapter event year after year.

Think of all the women out there who are talented with computers and can not only meet the needs of the chapter but soar with technology and make your chapter that much better! Think of all the women out there who LOVE spreadsheets and numbers... don't you want one on your team to help keep track of things? It is important to acknowledge the strengths of potential co-leaders and plug them into your chapter's roles, especially in areas where the founding leader is not as strong. It is also nice to have a friend dream with you and build your chapter together. You will be filled with ideas as your chapter grows and having a partner to live in that moment with you is just too valuable to deny!

We recommend each chapter have a leadership team consisting of the managing leader plus two co-leaders.

Roles and Responsibilities:

Managing Leader Roles and Responsibilities

❖ Completes all required training to establish, re-establish, or maintain established status of the local chapter

❖ Participates in ongoing support and training with the Chicktime National Organization, reaching out to the national organization for support when challenges arise, regularly review leader resources available on the Leader Resource menu at Chicktime.com

❖ Sets vision and inspires leadership team and volunteers (defines the expected direction of chapter-where you are going and how you are going to get there)

❖ Ensures all chapter roles are filled and carried out

❖ Facilitates Annual Leader Drive to ensure calendars are full prior to the beginning of each year. This includes the name of each month's workshop leader and the activity they plan to use.

❖ Plans and leads the monthly business meeting as part of every Chicktime Event

❖ Communicates vision of the Chicktime National organization and supports vision by ensuring chapter follows the Chicktime model, represents and fulfills the mission, and embraces leaders and volunteers interested in starting their own chapters

❖ Point of contact with the Chicktime National Organization

Individual Co-Leader Roles (may be split up among leadership team based on their talents and joys)

Volunteer Coordinator:
Leader Name-

❖ Reaches out and welcome new volunteers within 24 hours when you receive a notification.

❖ Checks personal email and make sure they received your chapter's invitations and, if not, let National know so they can troubleshoot.

❖ Makes sure to use a signup sheet at Chicktime events and emails or texts a pic of the sheet to us so we can add them to your database.

❖ Receives notifications when new volunteers sign up via VolunteerMatch.org. Sends a personal email welcoming them to the chapter, inviting them to the next Chicktime Event, and including a link to your chapter's website to view upcoming and past events to learn more about the work your chapter does and how they can get involved.

❖ Forwards all VolunteerMatch.org new signups to National so that the volunteers' contact info can be added to the CRM.

Website:
Leader Name-

❖ Manages website to ensure all content for all pages is up to date. Chicktime National will create and post your monthly invite and news pulled from the calendar and Facebook.

Facebook:
Leader Name-

❖ Take and collect photos and post them along with a cute write-up within 24 hours of your event. This person also shares fun posts about your charity partner and other events and volunteer opportunities they may have available.

Calendar:
Leader Name-

❖ Adds events to the calendar annually after the Annual Leader Drive (all 12 events) and updates the details as they become available or are changed.

Treasurer:
Leader Name-

❖ Manages chapter money. Inventories and keeps stock of Chicktime t-shirts and other gear. Orders new gear as needed.

Rising Managing Leader:
Leader Name-

❖ Agrees in advance to rise into the managing leader role when the time comes.

Shared Roles (managing leader and all co-leaders)

❖ Serve as co-host for equal number of Chicktime Events annually. Basically, this means dividing the 12 monthly workshops between the leadership team, and each leader takes responsibility for their share of the months. This includes: ensuring there is a qualified workshop leader for the months you co-host, familiarize yourself with your chapter's process to engage and retain workshop leaders (Engaging Monthly Leader Tool), use the Engaging Monthly Leader Tool beginning eight weeks prior to each event you are co-hosting to ensure the workshop leader is fully engaged, and the event runs smoothly, attend the month you co-host and be available as challenges arise, have back up activity ready to go in case there is a last-minute emergency.

❖ Embrace and support the vision of your chapter

❖ Familiarize yourself with your chapter's website and share it with others

❖ Embrace and support the vision of the Chicktime National organization- read our book, attend regional leader retreat annually, build and enjoy relationships with our National team, reach out to sister chapter leaders for support and offer support when you feel moved. It is very important for you to remember that we are here for each other.

❖ Build relationship with charity partner- ensure your chapter is meeting their promise of providing a Chicktime Event every month, be on time and if you are the co-host well organized for the event, when possible volunteer for the charity from time to time throughout the year, advocate for your charity by familiarizing yourself with their work and sharing it among your circles (familiarize yourself with their website and share it with others), at least annually (as a team) take your charity point of contact out to lunch, remember his/her birthday with a card, etc.

❖ Build relationships with volunteers – this naturally happens as your chapter consistently provides quality Chicktime Events monthly and a welcoming and inclusive culture is developed within your chapter. A fun lunch following a Chicktime Event at least once a year would be nice. In addition, you may consider hosting a book study, hiking group, lunch bunch, or any recreational activity you would enjoy the company of friends (old and new).

It is important to address the fact that leaders will come and go. This is totally acceptable and honestly a 'win' if she is being called into her next season! I do believe there is a graceful way to exit. The next chapter will address this in detail.

Chapter 8

What's Next?

Women move in and out of different seasons throughout our lives. Volunteering shouldn't be any different. It is so sad to me when a woman knows it is time to move on, yet guilt ties her to an organization. With that said, there is such thing as a graceful exit and I would like to share a bit about what that looks like for Chicktime.

We have many chapter leaders who start chapters, help lead them for while, and then move on to the next phase of their journey. I celebrate with each and every one. Some move into vocations in line with their life's mission, and they share with me that Chicktime helped reveal this next step to them.

Unfortunately, some start their chapters with great intentions and then a health scare or a family crisis intervenes. If chapters have strong co-leaders in place, the chapter can weather the storm, but if not, tabling the chapter may be the only option.

For either reason, there is a good and graceful way to exit. I've put together the following process as a guideline to consider when/if the time comes for you to move on.

The Graceful Exit

❖ First, counsel with husband, confidant, or someone who knows you well. Pray.

❖ Talk with your Rising Managing Leader and share it is time for you to step down and work out a transition plan for her to take over the responsibilities of managing the chapter.

- ❖ Call a meeting with your leadership team and invite potential leaders. This can be coffee, lunch, or just any relaxed place.

- ❖ Share your heart, where you are going next, and take a moment to share what you have learned from leading your chapter.

- ❖ Name the roles that you are 'seeing' for each on your team to fill.

- ❖ Leave plenty of time for discussion because you may find that they, too, have felt the call to move on, and you have effectively 'released' them to move to their next season by making the decision for yourself.

- ❖ During this meeting, work together to develop a strategic plan of how the chapter should move forward. If you are doing good work and have dedicated volunteers, you owe it to the chapter to figure out how it will continue.

- ❖ If there is follow-up needed, set up another coffee/lunch date before the meeting ends. It is important to establish goals and outline your plan of who will fill each role

- ❖ Make sure to stay on the chapter's roster and attend when you can. You will be blessed! And if you are the founder, you will forever be honored on your chapter's web pages as the chapter founder!!

Appendix

Chicktime Program Ideas

The idea is to expose everyone to a wide array of gifts so that they can look inside themselves and identify their own. They may find, through this process, that they love something that they didn't even know existed, or originally thought they wouldn't like.

Here are some fun ideas:

❖ Scrap booking: The workshop leader could lead the children in creating their own scrapbooks, or they could each create a page that would go into a scrapbook for someone else, like a military unit serving our country, a missionary group serving others or a cancer treatment center – just any group that needs encouragement, especially if the scrapbook pages were built around poems written by the children on the subjects of joy, peace, love, hope, etc.

❖ Creative writing: Maybe this should come before the scrap-booking!

❖ Singing: Our more musically talented members could bring their music group and perform a concert. They also could teach us a song, and we could practice the parts then sing it for the music group. Think how that song will resonate in all of our hearts, probably for a lifetime ... and bring us back to the love we shared with each other that day!

❖ Yoga ... Zumba ... ballroom dancing

❖ Sculpting

❖ Origami

❖ Volleyball, basketball or any other sport!

❖ Health and nutrition: Someone with a gift for explaining in easy-to-understand terms why junk food isn't our friend.

❖ Mini-conference: We all need empowerment from other women encouraging us to live better lives! If we don't have anyone in our group that feels her gift is ministry, maybe someone in our group has the power of persuasion and could encourage an incredibly inspirational women's leader to visit our group.

❖ Cooking classes

❖ Gardening

❖ Changing a tire or the oil for the car they will someday drive.

❖ Balancing a checkbook or hearing community leaders tell their stories.

❖ Pampering with manicures and/or pedicures.

These program ideas are only limited by the talents, gifts and passions of your volunteers!!

Fundraising

Chicktime, Inc. is a 501(c)(3) public charity.

Under the regulations set forth through our 501(c)(3) and the U.S. government, individual chapters are NOT authorized to issue a tax-deductible receipt for donations. Only donations processed through the Chicktime, Inc. 501(c)(3) qualify as tax-deductible donations. These receipts are issued from our national headquarters on an annual basis and will be signed by our founder and CEO, Lori Rhodes. If any donor receives a receipt other than that supplied by Mrs. Rhodes, it is not authentic, and we ask that you contact info@chicktime.com so we can assist you.

A bit more information:

Chicktime has designed a unique system for raising money for your charity partners. We basically encourage individual chapters to raise ALL major funds directly through the charities they serve. For example, if you see a need for a new playground, ask the home you serve if this is something they are interested in. Then raise the money with ALL checks/funds written directly to the home, earmarked with Chicktime in the memo so that the money goes toward the collaborative projects you and the home have agreed to work on. Simple!

The benefits of this fundraising model:

One, the beauty of tying women in the community to charities Chicktime serves on a deeper (financial) level is indescribable. Where your treasure is, your heart will be also! Having your donors write their checks directly to the charity knits a NEW tie between the local community and charity your chapter serves. The new donor will now receive news updates from the charity and will be listed in their annual report as a friend and supporter of the charity ... which is MUCH more powerful than having Chicktime collect the money and issue just one check.

Two, your chapter doesn't have the headache of collecting the donations, filling out forms, sending them to Chicktime National, tracking and following up with the funds, and all of the other paperwork that accompanies the processing of a 501(c)(3) donation.

Remember, your charity partner has full-time staff (or a staff member) that specializes in processing donations and they are HAPPY to do it!! We believe this is the best model for fundraising and highly encourage chapters to utilize this method.

With that said, individual chapters will occasionally need to process a large donation through the Chicktime, Inc. 501(c)(3). We can make this happen but please be aware that that the Internal Revenue Service places strict regulations on how 501(c)(3) monies are spent. These donations are handled on an individual basis, and all precautions are taken to ensure these large donations are tracked and spent for the intended purpose of the donor. Contact your local chapter leader if you would like to make a significant donation. Contact info is located on our website at Chicktime.com.

For general donation questions, please you may contact info@chicktime.com.

The concept is simple, really: Individual Chicktime chapters do NOT exist to raise money. Chicktime chapters exist to encourage women to develop their passions and use their gifts to help the broken, the lonely and for healing women and children in their local communities. The small amount of money it takes each month to provide a Chicktime program is easily manageable by the volunteer who has agreed to lead their workshop/activity ... she or her husband may have to work a bit of overtime ... ask her boss, a local business, family or friends to pitch in and donate supplies. This is all part of engaging the broader community ... and makes the local chapter that much more effective. If you don't believe it is possible ... think again. The Canyon Lake chapter has faithfully provided monthly Chicktime events with New Life Children's Center since 2007 and almost without exception, each monthly workshop/activity leader has provided all supplies needed for her activities without assistance from the local chapter!

Fundraising is covered in leader training. If you need a refresher, please contact info@chicktime.com

A Girl for God

by Laura Trujillo (teen volunteer)

Sitting in a church parking lot at 7:30 in the morning on a Saturday morning is not an ideal plan of action for a teenager; from personal experience, meaning that I am 18, I know that they would much rather be at home, asleep in bed until, oh say, about noon. But here I was with 15 other girls waiting to head out to go participate in this thing called Chicktime. I didn't really know what it was. I was just there because I am a senior, and therefore a leader of our Girls for God ministry, and my leader asked me to create and manage a station. At that point, I wanted nothing more than to just go home and go back to bed. On the drive over, Jennifer explained to us that the girls at this center had been relocated to there because their family background was not safe, and they put on a 'tough girl' persona, so we needed to mind all the rules and watch what we said/did. "Great," I thought to myself, "I get to go spend four hours with juvenile delinquents. Yay me." Little did I know that these girls would show me just how lucky I am and how great God is.

We pulled up, unloaded, were briefed on the happenings, and then escorted through a locked fence: not a very good sign in my mind. I proceeded to the room that I was assigned and set up my card-making station. The first group of girls came by, and I was a nervous wreck. I didn't know what to expect: Were they going to be nice? Closed off? Would they even participate? As time passed by and we got to talking with the girls, it was evident that these girls were just that, girls. They talked about who the cute celebrities are, who their favorite artists are, and about their school work. They worked diligently on their cards, all the while chatting happily with myself and the other girls helping. What really had an impact on me was a group of four girls. They had choreographed a dance but our CD player wouldn't play their CD. Instead of just sitting down and forgetting about their dance, they began to sing and dance. They had choreographed this dance specifically for our entertainment. These girls had spirit and creativity. They didn't let their past, current, or future situations handicap their fun.

These girls are at this place because something at home didn't go right and they got the bad end of the deal; yet, here they were singing and dancing, happy as can be. That's when I realized that on the outside, I was here so they could talk and interact with someone different and new, but in reality I was here to learn from them. They were teaching me that I should be grateful, happy and contented with my life. I have a loving family, a home, school and endless possibilities ahead of me. What I thought was going to be a waste of my time ended up as one of the best ways I've spent my Saturdays so far this school year.

The girls told us about certain activities Chicktime coordinated for them: a fashion show, a movie and a dance. We asked the girls what they wanted and our minds raced with thoughts. Jennifer asked if we would want to come back in the future and work with Chicktime some more and we practically screamed at her "YES!" As we loaded the van to head home, we were already talking about what we could do when we came back. Unfortunately for us, Chicktime is booked for the rest of the year and we will have to wait to return. Chicktime was something I needed. Something I needed to remind me just how fortunate I was. Something I needed to open my eyes and teach me how to be generous with my time and effort. I can honestly say that I would not change a single thing about the way I spent that Saturday.

www.ingramcontent.com/pod-product-compliance
Lightning Source LLC
Chambersburg PA
CBHW060637280326
41933CB00012B/2077